The Best Community Service Project Ever

by Joan Nichols

illustrated by Janet Skiles

Scott Foresman
is an imprint of

Glenview, Illinois • Boston, Massachusetts • Chandler, Arizona
Upper Saddle River, New Jersey

I guess you could say I'm pretty much a good kid, so it's difficult to understand how I got myself into this mess. Actually, it was AJ's idea. He's my cousin, kind of halfway between a brother and a friend, since we are only two years apart. We have lived next door to each other all of our lives. We were in middle school together—me in sixth grade, AJ in eighth. We were both looking forward to a long summer, before the trouble started.

Summer was only a day away, and AJ had just graduated from the eighth grade. To celebrate, he and three of his friends decided to paint some of the trees in the vacant lot near the school. They smeared KMS, which stands for Kingley Middle School, the year, and their initials all over the trunks. Usually I'm not welcome when AJ is with his friends, but this time he let me tag along to help carry the paint. It didn't seem like a bad idea to sneak out, slap on the paint, and sneak back home. We figured it might become a school tradition.

The only problem was that we got caught. A patrol car pulled up just as we were finishing. Everyone took off running at high speed. We might have gotten away too, except that I tripped and fell over a tree root, and AJ stopped to help me up. So he and I were left holding the empty paint cans!

Officer Yee said, "I could haul the two of you down to the station for this."

I have to admit I was shaking in my sneakers. I didn't think anyone would take our prank this seriously.

"But I know your parents and your school principal. I'll report this incident to Ms. Matthews tomorrow and let her decide what to do with you," Officer Yee concluded.

At nine o'clock the next morning, AJ and I were in the principal's office. Ms. Matthews, usually a pretty friendly person, wasn't looking very friendly at that moment.

"Dean and AJ, I'm surprised at you," she said.

"We didn't really hurt the trees," I said. "We just wrote on them with a little paint."

AJ chimed in. "And that place is a dump anyway. Who cares how it looks?"

"A dump, huh?" Ms. Matthews gazed out the window. Across the road was the vacant lot with its stagnant pond and scrawny woods. Splashes of bright red paint covered five of the trees.

"That gives me an idea. I'm assigning you a community service project. Clean up that 'dump.' You can begin this afternoon by scrubbing the paint off the trees. Then you can work on cleaning up the rest of the garbage."

"That will take forever!" AJ protested. "Summer football practice starts today."

I had planned on lots of summer hammock time before Mom sent me off to camp.

Ms. Matthews shook her head. "You should have thought of that before you took a paintbrush to those trees."

Early that afternoon, AJ and I were lugging rags, buckets of clean water, and boxes of trash bags to the lot. It looked even worse up close and in daylight. Tall weeds surrounded the pond. The water smelled terrible. Thrown among the weeds was every piece of junk you can imagine—fast-food wrappers, empty bottles, car parts, ripped plastic bags spilling rotting garbage, the wheels from a child's stroller, a broken light fixture, and rags everywhere. Old newspapers were draped on bushes and flimsy tree branches. It was a real dump.

The paint on the trees made it look even worse. It took us two hours just to scrub it off. The place was pretty quiet. All you could hear was the sound of our hands slapping at mosquitoes and the shouts from football practice in the field behind the school.

AJ looked grim. Summer practice was the one way high school freshmen could be sure of getting on the team once school started in the fall. AJ was a good player, but he needed to practice.

"Ryan, Stephanie, and Maria should be doing this with us," I said. "It was only luck they weren't caught too."

AJ shrugged. "Hand me that bag. We might as well start picking up some of this junk."

We worked in silence for a while under the hot sun. The cries from the field stopped. Practice was over. My knuckles were rubbed raw from scraping them against the tree trunks. My back hurt from bending over to pick up the trash. Sweat poured down my face.

I was just about to suggest we stop and get something cold to drink, when three bicycles raced up the street and screeched to a stop beside us. Ryan, Stephanie, and Maria stared at us with puzzled looks.

"How come you weren't at practice, AJ?" Ryan asked.
"Hey, wait a minute." He stared at the trees, now clean
except for a pinkish smear. "What happened to all our
hard work?"

AJ didn't answer. He just crossed his arms on his chest
and stared at them.

"You got caught," Stephanie said. "Is that it?"

AJ nodded.

"Um, did you mention our names?" Maria asked.

AJ shook his head.

"It's not fair," I said. "AJ had to miss football practice
to clean up this lot. You guys should help."

The three of them looked at each other. Then Maria
said, "Hand me a bag." A few minutes later all five of us
were hard at work.

Soon a jogger stopped to watch. "Hey, cool. Someone's finally cleaning up this mess. Awesome." She jogged in place while she talked. "I never noticed before," she said, "but look—there's a path here. You can hardly see it, it's so choked with weeds."

She bent over and yanked up a bunch of weeds. Sure enough, you could see the outline of a dirt path underneath. It went in the direction of the pond before it disappeared among the trees.

She held out her hand for a bag. "I'll see how much I can clear. It would be great to have a jogging path. Running in the road is scary with cars whooshing past."

"Wait a minute," I said. "Clearing the path isn't part of our job."

But AJ shushed me. "Let her help if she wants."

So I didn't say anything else, but she had me worried. Apparently, this was going to be a bigger project than I had planned on. I just wanted to clean up the trash and head home to my hammock.

We were beginning to attract a crowd. A man out walking his dog stopped to watch us. "Such good kids, cleaning up this lot."

"Hi, Mr. Diaz," the jogger said. Her name, she had told us, was Stacey.

He waved to her. "My wife and I live over there in the apartment complex." He pointed to a row of small apartment buildings on the other side of the pond. "We hate having to look at this garbage every day. I used to fish in this pond years ago. All the fish are gone now. I guess they couldn't survive here. It's too bad."

"Maybe they'll come back," I said.

"Maybe." But he didn't look hopeful. He walked off shaking his head.

Mr. Diaz got me thinking. I love to fish, but I have to wait for my parents' two-week vacation to go somewhere to do it. It would be great to have a place to fish in town.

Twenty minutes later, Mr. Diaz was back, pulling a shopping cart. A lady was with him. He introduced her to us. "My wife, Rosa," he said.

"I saw how hard you young people were working," she said, "and fixed you some sandwiches and cold drinks."

Just in time, I thought. With everyone helping us, we had managed to pick up all the trash. *Hammock, here I come.* We found places to sit and began munching on the finest ham and turkey sandwiches I had ever had.

"Gee, thanks, Mrs. Diaz," I said. "These are great."

"It's the least I could do when you're nice enough to clean up the lot. It's the mosquitoes I hate. A stagnant pond like this one breeds them."

Maria took a long pull of cold juice, took out a pencil and notebook, and started writing.

"What are you doing?" Stephanie asked.

"Making a list of what people want," she said. "Jogging path, fishing pond, mosquito control—" she looked up. "Hey, Dean, here comes your mom."

I turned around. Sure enough, there was my mom pushing my little sister Molly in her stroller and crossing the road from the school. "I've just been to see Ms. Matthews," she said. "She told me about your little incident."

I winced. Was she going to yell at me in front of everybody? But she just looked around and said, "This place looks better already. If there were a few benches, I could sit and watch Molly play."

I let out a sigh of relief. Maria added benches to her list, which was growing pretty long.

"Ms. Matthews said to tell you that she's proud of the job you have done," Mom said.

"What are we going to do with these?" Ryan pointed to the filled trash bags lined up along the curb. "We can't just leave them here."

Mr. Diaz took out his cell phone. "My son-in-law drives a pickup truck. He can haul them over to the dump."

Mr. Diaz put through his call. While we waited for his son-in-law to show up, Maria said, "Cleaning up this trash is just a start. People will be leaving more stuff here. This place doesn't look like a place to respect. It looks like a dump. Wouldn't it be great if it were a park with all these things that people want—fish in the pond, a path around it, benches?"

"And thick trees and shrubs," my mom added, "for shade."

"And flowers." Mrs. Diaz clapped her hands. "I miss my old garden so much. It would be wonderful to have flowers nearby."

"We could make the path around the pond a nature trail," Stephanie said. "And even put up signs telling what kinds of plants there are." Maria was furiously writing down every suggestion.

Without thinking about what I was saying, I got caught up in the spirit. "And a picnic table," I shouted. "Right under the shade of the trees."

AJ frowned. "Whoa," he said. "That sounds like a lot of work—and time."

He was right. What was I thinking? Summer was just about to start, and I couldn't desert my hammock like that. Still, it would be fun to fish in the pond.

"We wouldn't have to do the work," Stacey said. "We could propose the idea to the town council. Then, they could get the Parks and Recreation Department to do it."

"Of course," Mr. Diaz said. "Parks and Recreation. That's where my son-in-law works. Perhaps we can ask him what he thinks."

Everyone began talking all at once about the park. They pointed out different features that could be improved. I had to admit that all of it sounded like a pretty good idea.

Just then the truck pulled up, and we were introduced to Bruce Coleman, Mr. Diaz's son-in-law. He listened to our plan as we loaded the trash bags into the back of the truck.

"That's a great idea," he said. "But a project like that costs money for labor, equipment, and plants. Our department has been trying to get additional money for years, but we haven't been successful. So, good luck. I hope your plan works."

He drove off with the trash, and the rest of us decided the best idea was to have a committee present our plan to the town clerk. Somehow, Maria, AJ, and I were appointed to the committee. AJ grumbled, but Maria said, "It will only take a few minutes, AJ. Then you'll be free to go back to your football practice."

And I'll be free to go back to my hammock, I thought.

The town clerk's office was in the municipal building. The town clerk was very helpful. "The budget committee is meeting tonight," she said. "I'll mention your idea to one of the members of the council. Then the committee can vote on it."

"That's that," AJ said, as we walked down the steps of the municipal building.

"Are you kidding?" Maria said. "We have to be here tonight to show our support. We should try and get our parents to come too."

AJ groaned.

"You don't play football at night, do you?" Maria said.

"OK, OK," AJ said. "I'll be here."

"Me too," I said.

"Good," said Maria. "See you tonight, then."

The meeting room that night was packed. My mom was there, along with Maria's parents. My Uncle Jack, AJ's dad, was able to make it too. We all squeezed into a row at the back. "Your proposal is the last one on the agenda," Mom said.

Before that night, I never realized how many things the town has to spend money on—renovations to the library, repairs to the police patrol cars, and on and on. The school budget, my uncle said, was discussed at a separate meeting. On some items the council voted *yes*, on others, *no*.

The councilman who proposed our plan told about us kids painting the trees and getting caught—the whole story. I was so embarrassed I wanted to shrink into my seat. Thank goodness we were sitting in the back of the room.

When she finished, a Parks Department representative said, "This project would mean hiring additional staff."

"I don't think this town can afford it without raising taxes," a councilwoman said. I guess most people agreed with her, because our proposal was voted down.

"I guess that's that," I said, as we filed out of the meeting room into the hall. I'm back to the hammock. I did feel kind of bad about missing out on the fishing, though.

Just then a man with a notebook and pen came up to us and introduced himself. He was Tom Andrews, a reporter for the *Kingley Chronicle,* a weekly newspaper that my parents subscribe to.

"That was a great story about you kids trying to renovate the park," he said. "I'd like to write it up and take your picture for the *Chronicle.* I think our readers would be very interested."

AJ shook his head. "No way." I tried to hide behind my mom. We had gotten enough attention from this park, as far as I was concerned.

Maria pinched my arm. "Don't be silly," she hissed. "This fight isn't over yet. Maybe with some publicity we can get other people behind our project."

AJ and I were outnumbered. The reporter and the other adults agreed that publicity would be a big help.

Friday morning the *Chronicle*'s front page had a photo of AJ, Maria, and me—she's smiling, we are not—and the whole story under the headline: "Kingley Kids Fight to Bring Back Pond Park."

The publicity worked. It seemed as if everyone wanted to lend a hand. The Kingley Chamber of Commerce donated money. The Department of Public Utilities donated trees, fast-growing varieties like spruce and white pine along with red maples and willows. A group of people who worked in the local bank agreed to plant them. They also planted shrubs donated by our state's environmental protection department.

The Parks and Recreation Department used the Chamber of Commerce money to clean up the pond. Then they stocked it with fish.

A local printing company agreed to print up the signs we wrote for the nature trail. Omar, a guy in my class, volunteered his Boy Scout troop to clear and widen the path around the pond. Stacey's running club painted the bridge over the pond. AJ and I, along with Maria, Stephanie, and Ryan, pitched in as needed. Miriam Farhat of the Parks Department directed our work. Mrs. Diaz kept us supplied with snacks and cold drinks.

Ms. Farhat explained that we needed to provide a workable ecosystem. "Diversity is the key," she said.

She said the trees we planted would provide shade, control erosion, and provide nesting and resting stops for birds and small animals. Winterberry shrubs would look colorful and provide food for birds during the fall and winter. Flowering plants would attract butterflies and bees during the summer.

"We'll plant some of the trees right at the edge of the pond," she said. "They'll shade the water, cool the temperature, and help create a good habitat for the fish in the pond."

So our summer didn't go quite as we expected. AJ never did get to football practice, and I rarely had a chance to nap in my hammock.

On the other hand, when fall came, AJ made the football team after all. The work he had done in the park had made him strong, and he could throw and run just as well as the other kids.

I was in better shape than I had ever been. Mom cancelled summer camp, and I went fishing at Pond Park instead.

What is a community?

A community is any place where people feel responsible for each other and to the group as a whole. A town, a city neighborhood, even a school, church, or scout troop can be considered a community. Belonging to a community gives members certain rights and privileges, but it also imposes responsibilities.

A human community is like an ecosystem. Diversity can bring added strength as each member contributes his or her own abilities, talents, and perspectives for the good of the group.

What communities do you belong to? How have they helped you? How have you helped them?